For Robert MacNeil

We Don't Do Nothin' In Here

Ellen Turlington Johnston

Illustrations by
Virginia and Sean McMahan

MOORE PUBLISHING COMPANY
Durham, North Carolina 27705

Copyright 1976 by Moore Publishing Company,
Durham, North Carolina. All rights reserved.

Printed in the United States of America

Library of Congress Catalog Number: 76-46776
ISBN: 0-87716-076-7

First printing 1976
Second printing 1978
Third printing 1979

DEDICATION

This one's for you, North Mecklenburg High School! It is for the students, my fellow teachers, and the administration. It is for all of you who have accepted me for who I am, someone who marches, often haltingly, to a slightly different drummer. But you have seen that my heart is in the right place, and you *have* accepted me. I love you for that.

I will never forget what you, Mr. Joe Hunt, principal, said to me as we went over my evaluation sheet. You, Mr. Hunt, are logical, orderly, efficient. I am none of the above. You said: "Mrs. Johnston, I would not conduct a classroom as you do. But you are the teacher!" You gave me a very good rating, too!

Thank you, Mr. Hunt, Mr. Frank Gadsden, Mr. Bryce Hurd, for the respect and freedom you have given me.

Thank you, Mr. W.A. Hough, former principal, for the same thing.

Thank you, North Mecklenburg, for everything you have been to me, and for everything you have let me be.

With love,

Mrs. J.

PREFACE

I thought I was through writing about the world of school. I thought I had said it all in *So What Happened To You?*; that I was ready to write about other times and places and people and things. But poems kept happening in and around my classroom, and I kept writing them down, until – suddenly – *WE DON'T DO NOTHIN' IN HERE!* happened.

School *is* where it is happening for me. It is where it is happening, or not quite happening, or not happening at all for our young people. Yes, I found out I had a great deal more to say. About loneliness. About despair. About boredom. About reaching and touching, or not quite touching, or not touching at all.

I have tried, always, to be honest in my revelations about school, about my students, about myself. I have tried to show that a teacher must not only be a *teacher*; we must be human and honest, willing to reveal our vulnerability. We must not forget how to smile, how to laugh, especially at ourselves. Life is incredibly dreary for many young people today. Life can be dreary and discouraging, too, for us, their teachers. But I remember what Mr. W.A. Hough, former principal at North Mecklenburg High, used to say to us at faculty meetings: "If you do not give these young people a smile here at school, many of them will not get a smile . . . *anywhere*."

We must teach. We must touch. And we must love.

About the title: breathes there a teacher whose aim is to pique the imagination, stir the creative impulse, discover and *un*cover the child in the Cool Dude, breathes there such a teacher who has not been confronted, tormented with the classic: "But we don't do NOTHIN' in here!"

Enough said. Here it is – all of it . . . most of it, anyway – the unvarnished, unexpurgated truth.

P.S.
I am leaving North Mecklenburg High School and the regular classroom duties and interactions this year. Does that make me a hypocrite, one who speaks out of one side of my mouth as a dedicated teacher, then quits, negating all I bespeak? No! I am leaving one classroom for many. I will be going into classrooms throughout the state as a "poet-in-the-schools", touching young people, showing them that they, too, can see the world again through the eyes of wonder and joy of children; that they, too, are and always have been poets; that they, can *too* recreate their feelings, visions, and experience through words for others.

CONTENTS

Dedication
Preface
We Don't Do *Nothin'* In Here, 1
One of *Those* Days, 5
Our "Bell", 9
What Is This??? and The Christmas Limb, 11
To Whom It May Concern, 14
Reflections While Serving As a Judge
   For the Selection of the Cheer Leaders, 15
Right On, 18
They Worry About Me, 21
An Open Letter to the Young Student-Teacher-To-Be
  From a Nearby College Who Came to Observe My Fifth
  Period English Class Last Monday Afternoon, 26
A Pack 'A Tobacco, My L'il Ole Pipe, and *Me*!, 29
They Just Give the Prize For Your *Door*!, 31
I Will Never Know, 33
The Awakening, 37
And So I Passed..., 41
The Secret, 42
No Dancing In M-3, 44
All I Needed, 46
Tomorrow, I'll Do Better, 47
What Your Teacher's Manual Can and
  Cannot Do For You, 48
The Fall, 50
Check Your Preference, 53
He Who Laughs Last, 57
My! Aren't They Bright?!?, 61
The Trip, 63
It Was Here Not *Three* Days Ago!, 65
From the Fantasies Of a Not-So-Young-Anymore
  School Teacher, 69
Excuse the Interruption, Please..., 72
Who Said Today's Kids Don't Have Feeling?!??, 77

WE DON'T DO *NOTHIN'* IN HERE!

Today
a small sparrow
perched on a slanted window pane,
peeking, upside down, into my classroom.
Before I'd even seen the little eavesdropper,
three students shouted,
"HEY!
There's a POEM, Miz. J.!"
Sure enough, it *was* —
a real class-stopper.
They wrote in their "Polaroids,"
(the little note-pads
they take "word-pictures" in),
of freedom,
and boredom,
and upside-down,
and flight.
The poems sprouted
left and right.
About then, this voice piped up, loud and clear:
"I signed up for *English*.
When're we gonna do some ENGLISH in here?!?"

Today
we skipped backwards
to when we were very young,
and see-sawed,
and blind-man-bluffed at twilight,
and sang out OLLEY-OLLEY-OXEN-ALL-IN-FREE.
And I told them how
the principle happiness for me,
when I was six,
was my l'il Orphan Annie decoder pin.

Then, they remembered again
the wonder of home-made mud pies,
and magic wands that used to be sticks.
We wrote of tadpole pets
that — O! happy surprise —
turned to frogs . . . overnight;
and of floppity red-headed Raggedy Anns,
and three-wheelers,
and first patent-leathers shoes,
spittin' bright.
Children again, we spun our wonderment
into shimmering nets of words, there.
Again, the voice: "This is 'sposed to be *English*.
So when're we gonna ever do some ENGLISH in here?!?"

Today
we hobbled ahead
to very, very old.
We wrote of grandmothers,
great-uncles,
arthritis,
of tales told, told, and *re*told;
and of the musty smell of old,
and the thin-ness.
"His baggy trousers lapped around his ankles,"
Mary wrote.
When she read it to us, I got goose-bumply cold.
(So did quite a few others.)
We wrote about lonely . . .
"The eyes, outlets of many visions,
how tired and forgotten."
We wove words into tapestries of bony fingers,
trembling hands with brown spots,
and lavendar shawls.

Today
we played with words.
We found sixty-eight — count 'em — in all —
to use for "said,"
to show how someone *feels*;
like: they shout or exclaim or whimper or groan...
Words flew like confetti in there.
Then... the voice again... demanding:
"But when're we gonna have some *English*?"

"*English*?"

"Yeah. Nouns 'n adjectives.
Diagraming.
ENGLISH!
We don't do NOTHIN' in here!"

ONE OF THOSE DAYS

It is one of THOSE DAYS.
You know it when school begins,
 and a young man grins
 and asks, with a smirky glance:
 "You lookin' for rain, Mrs. J.?"
(Why DIDN'T you lengthen those pants???
 "High-waters" are *tacky*!)

First period.
 Somebody steals your Flair,
 the minute you look away.
 (It was your favorite pen.)
And then . . .
 your students clamor and shout:
 "WHAT notebooks???"
 when you say, "Get your notebooks out."
 (Why should *you* care?
 They couldn't write, anyway;
 they have no pens . . . or pencils,
  except for your favorite Flair . . .
   somewhere.)

It goes on downhill from there.

You type up a test on stencils.
You know that paper between?
That's what you fail to remove.
To show for the work you've done . . .
 three pages of blanks.

The outlook does not improve.

You leave your room during lunch.
You come back to find
 your decorations torn down . . .

    on the floor in a shredded bunch.
(You'd dressed your room up for spring,
    with streamers of pink and soft green.)
You try really hard not to mind,
    but it seems a very sad thing . . .
    you'd brightened your room for *them*!
        Some thanks!

The beat goes on this way,
    when a young man suddenly asks:
    "Why's your hair *orange*, Miz. J.?" . . .
      (You *only* cover the *gray*!)

Then you find out it's blue sheet day,
    the twentieth day, you know.
Your records quite clearly show
    it's only the *nineteenth* day.

About then, you remember this girl
    who went off with your last hall pass —
    and that was *three* hours ago!

It comes as a bit of a blow
    when the principal catches three students,
    (who are supposed to be in *your* class,
    under *your* jurisprudence,)
    smoking heaven-knows-what
    out there behind the gym.
    They say some bad words at him.
      (He thinks you really *should* know.)

It seems that things *may* look up
    when somebody brings in a toad,
    unloading him from a cup.
Delighted, you say: "Pretend
    that *you* are the hoppy toad,
    while giants around laugh and stare,
    and prod and poke you and goad,
    while you hop about on the floor.
    Now! Write about it for me!"

Like a cold, gray fog, APATHY
descends.
Your students stop laughing. Sit there . . .
and don't even care
about the small toad anymore.

THAT'S IT!
You'll hand in your papers – TODAY!

Until . . . .

A quiet person gets up from her chair
to sharpen her pencil.
She drops a crumpled note
on your desk, on the way.
You don't want to open it;
you're so afraid it will say:
"Why don't you get out,
while the getting's good.
I think you should."

But it says:

"Thank you for putting up with us."
And it says:

"I love you, Mrs. J."

You get a small lump in your throat.
Soft to yourself, you say:
"Oh well, Mrs. J.
It really *hasn't* been *such* a bad day!"

OUR "BELL"

We used to have a *nice* bell.
Sometimes you heard it.
Sometimes... you missed it.
Sometimes the kids would yell,
  "There went the bell!"
You would not discover
  that the class was not, indeed, over
      until...
  you'd dismissed it.
The kids would pour out, smartly smirking,
  knowing they'd pulled one more coup,
    (which, with that gentle knell,
      was *not* hard to *do*.)
Often, the principal would be out there, lurking.
He'd stem the surging throng
  before "recess" could begin;
  he'd herd them sternly back in,
    looking a bit unstrung.
I – wearing my sheepish-est grin –
  would try to make it clear
  that I thought that the bell *had rung*.
He'd be nice about it and say,
  "Yes, I know, Mrs. J.,
  That bell *is* a bit hard to hear."

Not long ago this year
  we got a new "bell."
It is *not* a bell;
  it is an ELECTRIC SHOCK.
It hits you with all the soft subtlety
  of a ragged rock.
It is a bit like that "BLEEP" you hear on TV.
  when they say: "This is only a test.
  In case of an emergency, contact your nearest.."
When it "rings" – that is, *blows*, it's
  for certain, *everyone* knows it!

I suppose we did need a bell,
   about which no one need be told
     that it's tolled.

  So . . . we've *got* it — and HOW.
     It is very TODAY.
     Unquestionably NOW.
     Decisive. Final. Cold.
        And LOUD.

We all should be very proud
   of the new, *now* "bell" we've got,
     and . . . . I'm NOT.

"WHAT IS THIS???"

"What IS this???

The bright young man squinches his thin nose,
   pursing lips across braced teeth;
   scowls, his brow contorted in almost-pain,
   and asks that I explain
      the form and classify
      the poem about our Christmas limb,
his voice grating . . . grim.

"What IS this?
   I cannot read it.
   I don't understand!"

(And it's quite plain
   he's not about to try.)

The verse he cannot read,
   or scan,
   or parse,
   or neatly stick a label on,
      offends.

"You read it to me," he demands.

And so I smile and read aloud to him
   the poem about our Christmas limb:

THE CHRISTMAS LIMB

A man was pruning the bushes at school —
   (outside of "C" hall,
      to make the place look tidy, trim, n' all.)

I asked could I have a limb.
He nodded agreeably —
(It was quite all right with him.)

I explained that the one I took
was to be our Christmas limb.
He gave me a funny look:
"You mean — your Christmas *tree*."

"Our Christmas *limb*," I said.
He quietly shook his head,
looking a teensy bit grim.

It's not the Christmas *mop**;
but still, it's really quite neat.
We leaned it against the wall,
the pencil sharpener its prop —
(as nice as you please).
It reaches four . . . five feet
across the top,
and looks sort of Japanese.

We tinsled, icicled it,
adding golden satin balls —
(from Family Dollar store.
At 69 cents a carton,
on sale,
I'd picked up four.)

The first time someone sees
our shimmery Christmas limb,
he or she will say:
"Why you do *crazy* stuff all the time, Miz J.?"

Many, concerned for me,
offer to bring a tree:
"You want a Christmas *tree*?
How 'bout I bring you one,
a little spruce, or a pine?"

---

*See "The Christmas Mop", *So What Happened To You?* (c1974) by Moore Publishing Company.

12

I tell them our Christmas limb
   is just fine . . .
   and more fun.

Now, most of the kids don't mind it.
   Fact is — more and more
   are 100% behind it!

Which goes, again, to show
   that a Christmas tree . . .
     the GLOW . . .
   is wherever you WANT to find it!

Too long, perhaps, and maybe too much rhyme,
Irregular, surprising when it comes.
No a b/a b; no a a/b b,
forms he's learned, and thus expects to find.
The language — a bit colloquial;
It doesn't *sound* like poetry — quite true.

And yet, as I read on,
   I watch his irritation fade away;
   I watch impatience softly wane to warm
     as he begins to hear . . . and understand
     what I've tried to show, in my own way.
   I see a tiny smile begin to play
   reluctantly, around his mouth; and then
   I watch it fanning full to easy grin.

"I think I get it now," he says.
 I think I like it, too."

Maybe . . . just maybe . . .
   the next time that he trips on something new,
   something he's not been conditioned to,
   he'll give a second glance and take a chance,
   hitch his trousers up and wade on in!

13

TO WHOM IT MAY CONCERN

I should have sent you Jimmy,
    the day that he cut class.

I should have sent up Mary,
    when she left without a pass.

But the office hassle can be grim . . .
    and drain a kid
    of what's left of him.

REFLECTIONS WHILE SERVING AS A JUDGE
FOR THE SELECTION OF THE CHEER LEADERS

The rating sheets place
COORDINATION first.
Then VOICE —
is it "resonant" and "loud"?
ENTHUSIASM and VITALITY
SMILE. POSTURE. POISE.
How will she look
leading cheers before the crowd?
TWO JUMPS required.
ONE CARTWHEEL and ONE SPLIT.
Then, at least one INDIVIDUAL STUNT,
(or more, if she sees fit).

We, the judges, who decide the fate
of the young girls spinning shiny dreams,
sit here stiffly in straight chairs and wait,
scanning the evaluation sheets.
With a flick-flick of a ballpoint pen,
five points here, three there,
check-check, check-check
we determine who will make the team.

Now they come — in threes,
tiny waists and pretty dimpled knees;
swishing, flirty hips and dimpled smiles,
swishing, shiny, flowing hair.

Give at least twelve points here
for the bouncy, bubbly blond,
smooth and agile — check.
Eight points for the vibrant voice. Check.
VITALITY? Oh yes! Oh my yes! Give her ten.

The redhead, more than graciously endowed...
   would she please the crowd?
Oh MY yes!! Yes *indeed* she would.
Give her nine for posture. POISE? Good!

The short brunette does back bends,
   rolling up into a limber ball,
   doing somersaults along the floor.
      Check-check. Check-check.

Pretty, graceful, mobile — one and all;
   swishy, slender, sassy — every one,
   each a XEROX of the one before.

Three groups down; two more groups to go.
There she is.
A skinny, floppy, ragdoll of a girl;
No chest, no waist, no hips to swish;
   her bony legs — parentheses.
The brown hair limply listless, scraggly, thin;
   the mouth . . . thin-lipped, set straight;
   scared, dull eyes,
   the kind that never really reach another's,
   but in shyness, always turn away.
She moves — a scarecrow among the others,
      duck-footed, hesitant.
The others raise the left hand; she — the right.
Turn a CARTWHEEL? Do a SPLIT? She can't.
Her turn to lead the cheer.
      VOICE?
How many points can you give
   for that pinched, tiny wail,
   strangely empty, hollow?
      COORDINATION?
When she jumps, her legs don't want to follow
   the rest of her.
Her arms — two sticks that flail,
   tiny windmills fanning at the air.

16

How many points?
You scan the sheet . . .
   nothing allowed for courage here;
   not a check allowed
   for fighting out against the odds,
   for trying, amid astonished stares
      of pretty, lithesome sprites.
No points given here
   for challenging the gods,
   who, doling out their gifts,
   presented her a hand of losing cards.
No points given here for one who has
   no beauty and no skill; yet, unawares,
      she struggles.
   And 'though she *has* to know she can't . . .
      she dares.

RIGHT ON

A girl drops by to talk a bit.
I notice she has a spot, a white dot,
   a *thing*,
   there on her nose.
At first, I do not mention it,
   thinking it will go away.
   But it does not.
So, after a little while, I say:

   Edna,
   you have a spot, a white dot,
      a *thing*,
      there on your nose.

She answers, with condescending smile.

   Yes. I know.
   It is not a spot, a dot,
      a *thing*.
   It is an ear ring.

An EAR RING? On your NOSE?!?

She says: So — where've you been?
It is RIGHT ON. The latest style.

Swiftly, she pulls it out, and then,
   deftly, reinserts the thing
   through the pierced place where it goes.

I wince.
   It looks . . . uncomfortable . . . to me,
      with that sharp pin sticking in.
I'll bet it tickles the small hairs in her nose.
What, I wonder, happens when she blows?

Besides that, it looks DUMB,
no matter how aesthetically
I try to view it;
no matter what angle I view it from.

But it's RIGHT ON. Their *thing*.

So — hundreds, even *thousands* more will do it...
I suppose —
wear an ear ring on their nose.

THEY WORRY ABOUT ME

I thought for a long while
   they were kidding.
They'd say,
   "You're crazy, Miz J."
I'd just smile.
I didn't take it as a slap,
   only a small love-pat.

But . . . I wonder . . .

I tap-danced, just a step or so,
   one day . . .
   to show them how Shirley Temple
   used to dance like that.
   (She was my hero.)
It embarrassed them, though.
They snickered softly —
   and not so softly.
Someone said to someone near,
   "She's CRAZY!"
I pretended not to hear.

I jumped in the leaves last Saturday.
See . . . we raked and raked,
and piled them high.
So, under an autumn sun
   and a cool blue sky,
I took a running leap,
landing in the middle in a heap.
   It was fun . . .
   with the leaves in my hair . . .
   and everywhere.
I told them about it on Monday
   and recommended it to them —
      highly.

Someone said to someone —
    wryly,
"That lady is a real *dingbat*, man!"

Of course, we have a jack o'lantern in my room
    every Hallowe'en,
    and tell ghost stories, besides.
They think that's crazy kid stuff.
But, I notice, when we turn the lights off,
    and that candle inside
      pierces the gloom . . .
    they like it well enough.

Then . . . there *was* my Christmas mop.
They thought that was crazy, too.
    But, I notice, they brought their friends
      to stop
      and look at it a lot.

And I do award a Snickers bar sometimes,
    or a chocolate kiss,
    or Doublemint gum,
    for the best Haiku,
    or the realest character,
    or the most *good* verbs.
It's a bit like when you feed peanuts
    to the bears at the zoo.
You toss the winner the prize,
    and he smacks his lips while the others
      look hungrily on.
        Crazy?
But when all's said and done,
I notice they do some of their best writing then.
And, I notice, he who wins doesn't surmise
    that I'm so very crazy!

I have this bauble.
    It's pink . . .
      a very PINK plastic ring,
        the size of a large marble.

(I won it playing Skee-Ball at the Fair.)
  It's something I wear
    quite a lot.
People who like me, tell me
  I should NOT.
People who *don't* like me
tell me the same thing!
But *I* like it.
So . . . I wear my Skee-Ball ring.

Then . . . there's my pipe.
I have this little pipe I'm terribly fond of.
  I puff on it sometimes,
    and they know I do.
  They think that's crazy, too.
Once, I told them the little poem I wrote about it:
  "A Pack 'a Tobacco, My L'il Ole Pipe, and Me."
That didn't help a whole lot, either.

Last Hallowe'en, I went out for a breather,
  dressed up like an old man,
    with a wig and a top hat.
I didn't ring any doorbells —
  nothing like that.
I just strolled the streets.
Sometimes, I stopped
  and smiled at the spooks.
    And I helped a little goblin pick up his bag of sweets,
      caramels and peppermints,
        that he'd dropped.

I was more than content,
When I told them about it,
    they looked at each other — funny,
    and shook their heads.
I heard "Crazy"
    "Crazy . . ."
    "Crazy . . ."
  ripple through that room
  like a soft breeze through a field of wheat.

I talked to my lecturn today.
It's so old and tired — my stand,
  crooked, beaten, bent.
It's seen better days, you might say.
  (Once, I asked them what they would compare it to.
  Someone said: "To YOU, Miz J."
  And I guess that wasn't far from true.)
Well, I patted it gently,
And told it to "hang on in there, baby,"
  (like the song says).
Why not . . . for heaven's sake?
We all need a word of encouragement, now and then.
  They whispered among themselves,
    and looked at me — funny . . . again.
One of my good young friends said softly,
  "Miz J., I worry about you.
    You *are* crazy!
    You just talked to your *stand*!"

    "I know," I said.
"We all need a word of encouragement, now and again."

You know, I *used* to think they were kidding.
Now . . . I think they're worrying . . .
  I really do.
But I also think . . . between me and you . . .
  they — sometimes — *envy* me just a bit, too!

AN OPEN LETTER TO THE YOUNG STUDENT-TEACHER-TO-BE
FROM A NEARBY COLLEGE WHO CAME TO OBSERVE MY
FIFTH PERIOD ENGLISH CLASS LAST MONDAY AFTERNOON

Dear Young Man,

I hope you are all right now. You did not look well when you left my classroom last Monday afternoon. You looked grim and pale.

I want to explain something to you, because I know you were expecting to observe something a bit more traditional, more structured, in the way of an English class. You see, I had *promised* my eleventh graders I would read from my diary to them on that particular Monday, the diary I kept when I was in the eleventh grade. I did try to persuade them that we should put it off until Tuesday . . . remember? I could sense that you were not ready for it. But remember, too, how disappointed they were, how they anxiously, sternly, overwhelmingly reminded me: "But you *promised*, Miz J.!"

A promise *is* a promise, isn't it? How could I let them down?

You, Young Man, sat at a desk, stiff and uncomfortable, your neat black note book rigidly before you, your pen firmly in hand. I did not want you to feel stiff and uncomfortable. Remember how I smiled reassuringly at you, suggesting, perhaps, you not try to take notes this time? But you did not put your pen down. You did not smile.

As you'll recall, I got out my little red diary, then, and read aloud about the adorable, popular Archie, whom I loved passionately and unrequitedly all during my junior year in high school.* My eleventh graders liked the part where Archie, the campus Romeo, took me to the school dance and at midnight, when the lights came on, there was my dad,

*See "Archie", *So What Happened To You?* (c1974) by Moore Publishing Company.

hurrying toward us, saying gently, but firmly, "It's time to go home now, Ellen," and about how I died a million humiliating deaths right there on the gym floor.

They loved it. Remember how they laughed?

But you, Young Man, did *not* laugh. You looked grim. Confused. Miserable. What would you, *could* you, tell your education professors, your peers, about THIS?

As if *that* weren't bad enough, my students decided you should hear my poem about my pipe. "Do it for him, Miz J.!" they clamored. I could tell you were not ready for that, either. But they wanted to share it with you. So I did it for you. And I tried to do it well, the way they like it, with me beating out the rhythm on my lecturn between stanzas, with expression and all. As I was reciting, my eleventh graders beamed, looking from me to you to me and back to you, just as a young mother searches the face of an on-looker when her two-year-old is doing something she deems remarkable and she seeks a reflection, an affirmation, of her own pride and delight. They wanted so for you to like it, to enjoy it. They were so proud. Honestly, I don't think they even noticed your discomfort.

I apologize, Young Man. I do not know what you wrote in your black notebook that day, nor how you explained my English class to your professors and peers. I do hope you feel better now. I wish you well with your student-teaching. I wish you joy and laughter and love in your classroom.

With love,
Mrs. J.

P.S. I enclose a copy of my pipe poem, just in case they didn't believe you back in your education class.

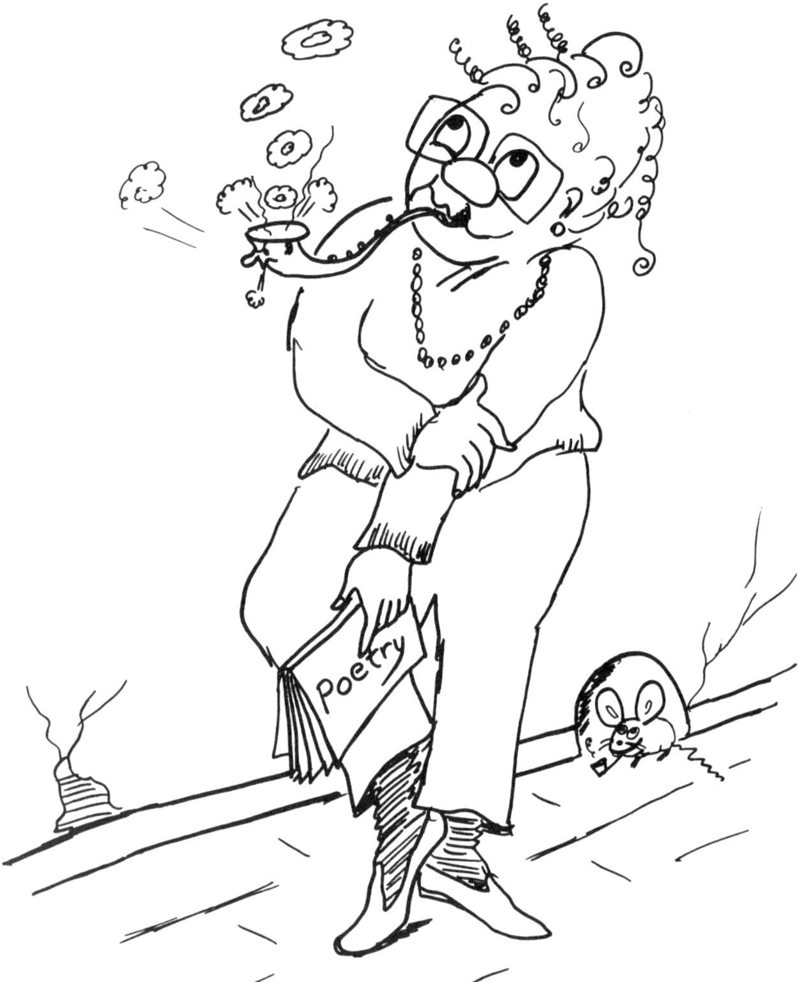
Poetry

A PACK 'A TOBACCO, MY L'IL OLE PIPE ... AND ME!

I was at this party the other night.
Everythin' was goin' all right,
We was tellin' jokes, talkin', laughin', and stuff.
It appeared to me the time was ripe,
So I took it out and LIT UP my pipe;
Before you know it, I'd taken me a GOOD puff!

You'd a thought I'd dropped an atomic bomb.
Like before a storm, there was a turrible calm.
They looked at me like I was some kind of a freak.
So I ups and says, "I got no regrets.
I threw away all my cigarettes.
I reckon I been smokin' this pipe now about a week!"

Well, my boy friend turned to me and said,
He said, "Baby, you MUST be outta' your head."
He said, "That ain't the way a lady's 'SPOSED to do."
He said, "You gotta be kiddin', but it don't look good.
He said, "Put down that pipe. I mean, I wish you would.
If you don't pretty baby, you and me is all THROUGH!"

Well, that made me MAD, and that's no joke.
A lady's gotta have somethin' to smoke;
If it ain't cigarettes, what is it gonna BE?
'Seems to me it'd be worse, by far,
If I was to smoke a big black cee-gar,
And chewin' tobacco just don't APPEAL to me!

I 'spose I *could* take to sniffin' snuff,
But I don't believe I'd like *that* stuff.
Besides — who wants to go sneezin' around all day?
I'M EMANCIPATED. I'M FREE AS AIR.
AND I GOT MY RIGHTS, and it don't seem fair
For a fella to talk about a gal with a pipe that-a-way!"

He said to me, "Baby, this is IT!
You take one more puff and I'm gonna quit."
He said, "It ain't lady-like; it's a downright pure disgrace."
He said, "BA-A-A — by, what's it gonna be . . .
Gonna be that pipe or is it gonna be me?"
So I took a B - I - G puff. . . .
    and I BLEW IT. . .right. . .in. . .his. . .FACE!
Now I'm all alone; what's done is past.
I got no more friends; I'm what you call "outcast",
'Cause I stuck to my guns, and I stuck to my pipe, you see.
I get lonely sometimes, but I got no regrets.
And I'll never go back to cigarettes.
It's just a pack 'a tobacco . . .
    my l'il ole pipe . . .
        and ME!

"THEY JUST GIVE THE PRIZE FOR YOUR *DOOR*!"

> We sat there
> complaining a lot,
> as everyone does
> that time of the year:

> "Christmas is NOT
> what it *was*!"

> "I can't get the spirit!"

> "Whatever happened to Christmas *past*?"

> We whined,
> "I'm not ready.
> Christmas comes 'round too *fast*!"

> . . . . .

But one day . . . . .
  we made some poems
  for the old, sick people,
  who haven't felt that Christmas *is* what it *was*
> since they were put away
> in the Home.

> We printed the verses,
> and drew pictures for them with sparkly stuff on.

Then we felt like fixing our room.

We looped silvery tinsel all through
  the light fixtures there,
  'hung icicles and sparkly things
> everywhere.
  (It looked a bit cluttered,
> but shimmery . . . beautiful, too.)

31

Someone came in and asked:
"What've you got all those pictures
with sparkly things on them for?"

and . . .

"Why'd you fix up your room?
They just give the prize for the *door*!"

Softly we said: "*We* know . . . "
and just smiled,
snugged in our Christmas glow.

I WILL NEVER KNOW

You and I —
we used to laugh a lot.
You brought me little things —
a poem you wrote,
a poster with a butterlfy,
an orange plastic ring
 from your box of Cracker-Jack.
'Til that day in class we talked of how
some Blacks don't . . . can't believe —
 not yet . . . not now —
that it *is* beautiful —
 this being black.
(Cicely Tyson said that
at the Convocation we went to.)
They were raised, she'd said,
in a world of white,
where standards decreed black skin
 not beautiful, not "in";
 the same for kinky heads.
So they patent-leather hair,
try to make skin light.
Some Blacks, Miss Tyson said,
are not yet truly freed,
and not yet proud
of their place in the sun.

"I was not raised that way!
I was taught I'm good as anyone!"
Your brown eyes, flashing hate;
your voice piercing, loud,
 slicing at me through the room.

 "Wait!

That is good," I said.
"But it *is* hard for some to overcome
 things they were taught.

Some, who still are caught
   in false beliefs,
 and some, who still can't feel
   that Black *is* beautiful,
     won't wear Afro's.
And some, who can't believe,
   wear giant Afro's,
   and shout -- in tones of steel:
     Black IS beautiful!
     BLACK is BEAUTIFUL! ...
   to drown false cries within,
   and put light powder on their skin."

Then you turned on me:
   "How would you feel --
     always being turned away
     because you're black?
     How would *you* feel if you'd come home one day
     and found your father hanging from a tree?"

"I understand," I said, "the way you feel.
   But don't you see?
 I am ashamed of cruelties before --
   all those things were true.
 But they don't happen anymore.
 Can't I help, now, make it up to you?
 I understand what it must be --
   blackness hating white.
 I dreamt that I was black one night.
   I hurt. I hated.
 I dreamt I tried to cover up black skin
   with powder. I could not.
     (The day before my dream, I'd seen
     a Black, a teacher, putting on a lot
     of powder to try to make her light.)
Believe me, I *do* understand."

While I talked, you wrote.
Here is what you handed me that day:

" 'I understand,' you say.
   You see how we feel.
  So you say, and I *know* you do.
  You sit in the front of the bus all your life.
  We sit in the back.
  But still *you* understand.
    Sure you do.
  While you were watching movies in the Carolinas,
    we were watching the 'Whites Only' signs.

"Sure," you'd written, "*you* know how it feels.
  You understand how it is to stand
    and wait in line for a job,
      and be turned down because you're the wrong color.
  You tell *me* I'm ashamed of my blackness.
  You tell me I'm not as good as white,
    my kinky hair should be straightened.
  I suppose you think by telling me you can make me believe it.

And just to think, I was about to believe
    that Black was beautiful,
    and things had changed . . ."

I read your words – aloud.
  But as I spoke . . .
  my voice broke . .
  words all swam together there.

A white voice spoke up then,
A poet, visiting my class, asked her:
  "Don't you think that you
    have gone too far?
  I don't think you've been fair.
    Things *are* better now.
  Though," he added, "I'll allow
    a lot of whites, it's true,
    'Liberals' pretend
    in name alone to be the black man's friend."

You pointed, then, at me.
Oh God, I can't erace
   the way you looked — your face . . .
      the curled lip . . .the sneer . . .
    the hate.

And — for the first time, then — I understood.
    I knew.
  Soft, I said to you,
    "I was wrong —
    me with my white face,
      straight hair —
    wrong to dare
     to say I know.
    I never could.
  I am not black, and I will never know.

Believe this one thing, though . . .
I didn't just *pretend*,
    I really am your friend.
Above all — *this* is true."

I looked up . . .
    and you were crying, too.

THE AWAKENING

We had this talent show.
We called it "Together."
   And it *was*.
We had
  songs...
  and skits...
  drama... dance...
  and more.
    HITS!
And a BIG band
  with vocalists
    who handsomely wore
    sleek scarlet suits,
    with tight satin pants.
    TOGETHER!
    We "got it ON!"

We carefully screened all the acts,
  so they'd be "top drawer,"
    and tasteful,
    and nothing would get out of hand.

We screened all the acts... except one.
This young lady, who tried out with a young man
  for the Dance contest part of the show,
    was VERY good.
She had the agiles,
  and the mobiles,
  and all the moves a dancer should.
She could do the limbo...
I mean — she could make her whole *body*
  parallel to her knees, you know,
  and walk around that way.
    Incredible!

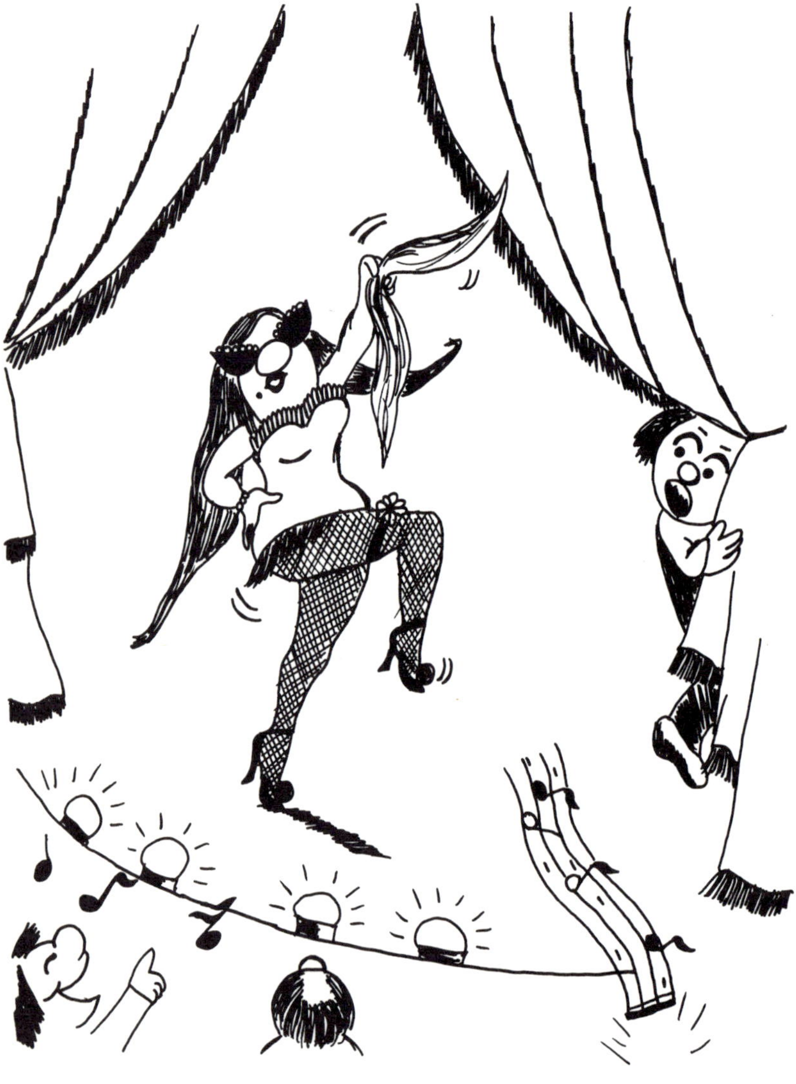

At the last minute before we drew up the program,
she asked could she do a "Creative Dance,"
    solo.
I said "O.K."
  It didn't seem to be taking a chance,
    for she was a lovely young lady,
      everyone said so.
      Quiet. Demure. Shy.
  (They told me her mother was *very* strict with her,
    which explained why
      she was so demure . . .
        and quiet . . .
        and shy.)

Her dance came on half-way through.
I missed the start of it.
  (I was out in the hall, in fact,
    when she commenced her act.)
I returned to the wings,
  and heard whistles and wolf-calls and things
  that people don't usually *do*
    for a *"Creative* Dance,"
    nor for any part of it . . .
    not even when it's *very good*.
The young men back stage were watching,
  and choking in short, gaspy pants,
    "I can't take much more!",
  as they shoved one another aside, so they
  could.

I, too, looked out from back there.
In my first frozen glance,
I perceived wriggling, writhing, contorting HER,
  making moves that *I* never knew *were*!

One trembling young man wheezed weakly,
  "She shouldn't be doing THAT . . . *should* she?"

    I nodded – mutely,
      feeling the same thing . . . acutely.

Indeed, *this* was no "*Creative* Dance."
Our prim young *prima donna* was doing a DIRTY dance.
And that captive audience: those mothers —
   not hers, but others,
   and nice little sisters and brothers,
   were getting a whole lot more
     than they bargained for!

(Thank goodness, HER mom wasn't there.
   She'd not have considered it funnery.
   She'd have got that poor girl to the nearest nunnery.)

Now, here's some advice: and it's sage:
All ye talent show sponsors, BEWARE
   of quiet, young, shy Innocence.
For, bathed in the spotlight's glare,
   beyond Mama's hovering care,
   finding its place in the sun,
   up on that glittering stage —
     before God and everyone
   it bumps and grinds and lets down its hair . . .
     and relentlessly comes of age!

AND SO I PASSED . . . .

A girl — quiet, skinny, small —
crouched in a corner in a hall
behind a door, staring straight ahead.

"You'd better move," I said.
"Don't you think you should?
Somebody might step on you."

She didn't move.
She didn't smile.
"I only wish they would."

I need to talk with her a while.
I needed very much to stay.

    I really wanted to.

But I was late for class.

And so I passed . . .
and hurried on my busy, busy way.

THE SECRET

The first time I ever saw her
everything in me winced.
A tiny, shriveled, shrunken woman-child;
pain in faded eyes etched deep,
a face steeped in despair.
Acne-scarred; scarred and thin and gray.
So homely that others looked,
and looked away.

Day after day, she dragged in, took a chair;
No light, no life. She just sat limply there.

What was it made her finally turn to me?
Was it the day we talked about our masks,
 the way we build facades to hide our pain,
 so others cannot know the hurt within?

She came to me — when everyone had gone.
And so it tumbled out, that avalanche
 of pain, not being wanted, lonely fear;
 shuttled back and forth — from home to home,
   not wanted anywhere.
   Would she hang on to life?
   Or would she just let go
  of toppling cliffs to which she barely clung?

The thing she did not know.
The thing nobody knew
 was that I, too, just barely hung
 to those same crumbling cliffs;
  my world — just blown apart,
  my dreams — all crumbled, too.
I masked *my* anguish with a voice too loud,
     a smile — too bright.

I knew, then. I knew that it was right
to open up the secrets of my heart
to this small, lonely, hurting woman-child.

And so, I told her there
of secret torments, too, in me.
It was the way . . .
  the way to show her that I knew . . .
  could *feel* what lonely is . . .
              and what despair.

When she came back that day,
  something had happened.
Her face had changed; the hard lines – gone.
Instead, a softness there, an almost glow.
Gone from her the blank, dull, awful gray of . . .
          isolated lonely nothingness.
        Very soft to me, she said:
          "To have somebody care
          so much that they would share
          a secret – such as you have given me . . .
        I never had a friend like that before."
And then – she smiled . . . all soft and warm and love.

Some teachers like to say:
"Keep your distance. Don't let down at school."

I thank God that I threw away that rule.
For . . . reaching out – we touched.
      And touching – grew that day.

NO DANCING IN M-3

Spread the word.
Tell the gang you've heard
    that there will be
    no more lunch-time dancing in M-3.
Not for a while, now.
First, I have to overcome my sad.

Ask them was it worth the kicks they had,
    breaking in my room — somehow;
    pushing, rushing, scrambling to get out
    as I returned . . . quite unexpectedly;
    leaving papers scattered in their rout,
    trying to escape before I'd see?

Just *ask* them: was it worth the sad
    they brought on me?

I was glad to share my room at lunch
    for dancing everyday.
I'm gone ten minutes one day so the bunch
    breaks in to dance while I'm away.
    "Just wait," I'd asked them, "I will be back soon."
    But they broke in the minute I was gone.

"That's no BIG DEAL," they'll say.

To me — it's a *BIG* deal.

Tell them I said it's small things that reveal
    the thing which is most true.

Tell them I said: "I love . . . I trusted you,
    and tried to help you have a little fun
    in my room, my home away from home.
    Look where it got me, all my trust undone."

Tell them I said: "You *used* me, sometime friends,
for your own pleasure-grasping ends."

Ask them to give me just a little while
to come to grips with this reality,
the way things *are*,
not the way I'd like for them to be.

I gave them inches, and they took the mile.

They'll have to give me time . . . some days . . . a while . . .

Please tell them, then,
maybe I can open up the doors again
for dancing in M-3.

ALL I NEEDED

Magnolia.
   Porcelain perfection.
   Ivory velvet.
     Exquisite . . . unreal.
I share it with third period.
   Look!
   Smell!
   Touch it . . . gently . . . *gently.*
Oh, let *my* wonder be yours.
Know the heart's catch I feel.
   Share my delight.
Oh please, somebody. DO.
I pass it among you.
   Someone pinches it.
   Someone snickers.
Someone — don't tell me who —
rips off a petal or two.
Then, softly, someone whispers,
   "It feels like a puppy's ear."

I smile.
I can go on that *quite* a while.
I will be all right.
   ". . . like a puppy's ear,"
is all I needed to hear.

"TOMORROW, I'LL DO BETTER"

"He turned without a signal."
"He passed the bus."
"You should have seen the car," somebody said.

Just yesterday
   he sat here in my classroom . . . over there.
I scolded him; he wasn't listening.
   (I'd asked a question, which he had not heard.)
He answered, sort of smiling, sheepish then,
   "I will not talk again.
     Tomorrow I'll do better" 's what he said.
He ran a hand through tousled, yellow hair,
   wrapping loose, long legs around a chair.

"A transfer truck," somebody said.
"He was really speeding," was the word.
"Following too close, he didn't look."

And so the stories spread.

What's the difference? Now he is dead.
And yet, I find I cannot take my pen
   and cross his name from my attendance book.

WHAT YOUR TEACHERS' MANUAL
CAN AND CANNOT DO FOR YOU

When I first became a teacher,
There was one thing I would reach for
As the students took their places, turned their faces up to me.
If I hadn't — well, I knew that
I'd be thrown in such a stew, that
They'd *know* I didn't know it all; I'd lose supremacy.

So my manual I'd hide there
In my text, or to the side there,
So they never would discover where I got the answers from.
I'd skillfully conceal it;
With guide close by, I'd feel it
Wouldn't be uncovered I was — sometimes — *almost* dumb!

It was my strength, my Bible.
I never deemed it liable
To be anything but accurate, inviolate, and true.
I'd eagerly peruse it;
For each question I would use it,
Taking little sneaky peeks when we'd come to something new.

Should I not have had this crutch by
For questions in the clutch, I
Knew I'd falter, stumble, be a laughing stock, turn red.
When they didn't answer right, I'd
Pull the old reins tight, I'd
Shout: "You're WRONG!" (That wasn't what my manual had said.)

But then one day, I groped for
My manual; I hoped for
An easy-going, cut-and-dried, 'go-round with *Moby Dick*.
It wasn't *there*! I clasped my
Throat; my voice rasped, I
Felt the classroom spinning; I grew nauseous and sick.

I knew it would be rough, but
I held out for a bluff, but
Feared I was too devastated, harried by my loss.
'Till suddenly the notions
Came tumbling in like oceans.
Freed! . . . the Mariner — I — as he shed his albatross.

An albatross that strangled.
Now, new ideas — bespangled —
Danced ahead like white caps; I could see them, feel them, too.
The waves of thought rolled in now;
Excitement could begin now;
Let it come — the unexpected different slant, the new!

Queequeg we compared to
Ones we knew; we fared, too
Splendidly with Ahab, (old Peg Leg), and the Whale.
We dove into discussions
With rippling repercussions
That Melville never dreamed someone could fish up from his tale!

It's not I'm not beholden
To manuals, for golden
Truths abound within their little pages by the score.
It's just — there's so much *more*, you
Reach out and explore, you
Charter your own voyages; no limits anymore.

So now, when someone comes up
With something NEW that sums up
A theme, perhaps, or character . . . I hardly ever hedge.
"It doesn't say so *here* but
I think your point's clear. Let's
Say, between my guide and you, by George, YOU'VE got the *edge*!"

THE FALL

I felt really good today
in my pant suit — new.
The top is greenish-blue,
which everybody says
is MY color.

That's right:
Three students told me *before* the first bell,
"Mrs. J., *that* is YOUR color!

I was something to see
up there in front of my class,
looking *and* feeling exceptionally well.

CONFIDENCE — that was me.
POISE? Yes!
COCKY? Almost.
(Not *really* . . . . but *almost*.)
The toast
of the school.

But — — — — a fool.

For in third period, a young lady, gently beckoning,
provided my moment of reckoning.

I had been telling them that wonderful myth
of Orpheus and lovely Eurydice.
When you tell that tale
your arms flail,
emphatically,
dramatically.

I was in my element, all right.
On top of things. Bright.

That's when the young lady beckoned me near,
whispering soft in my ear,

"Mrs. J., you've got a BIG rip under your arm."

WHERE???!!!???

"Shhhh," she whispered. "Under your arm. There!"
Embarrassed for me, she sought to explain.

My poise, my confidence took wings
And soared — — — — — — — right down the drain.

If I could have, I'd have gone up in the air
like so much powdered chalk there.

My bad arm pinioned to my side, I racked my brain:
"When did I shave last?"
It came to me then, God forbid.
It was a week ago Tuesday — past,
And here it was — Wednesday . . . *next*.

I was sinking — fast . . . .

and . . . SUNK . . .
I slunk.

I wasn't on top of things anymore.
I wanted only to be *under* things,
or *in* things.

I wasn't bright, like before,
and not even very nice, then,
as I had been,
and from there on, promised me
I SHALL BE!

For I asked them; nay, I begged them,
almost on bended knee.
(Not really . . . . but *almost*):

51

"Listen, people, if you ever ever *ever*
see a run in my stocking . . .
DON'T TELL ME!
If my pants are split,
or my shirt doesn't fit,
or is splattered with grit,
and you're aware of it . . .
DON'T TELL *ME!*
"Yea, 'though my face be covered in jam,
Please, dears, just let me be what I THINK I am!"

CHECK YOUR PREFERENCE

A marvel it was!
Topics, sub
  and sub;
  over,
  under.
As outlines go — a wonder.
On yellow paper, neat and bright.
A school teacher's delight.

They put it in my box.
It said:
  "PROPOSALS OF THE FELLOWSHIP COMMITTEE
  The wishes of the majority will be carried out.
  Please indicate by checking your preference regarding
    each item."

So – – – – all right.
I read on.

          "OCCASIONS FOR REMEMBRANCE

ILLNESS

1. Member
   A. In the Hospital
   ___ Flowers
   ___ Candy, etc.
   ___ Fruit
   ___ Toiletries

   ___ Get well card
   ___ Other suggestions"

My suggestions?
Just one thought: "If I am sick," I wrote,
                  "I think it would be nice
                    to get a little, unexpected note."

"B. At Home (after one week)

    __ Get well card   __ Gift (handkerchief,
    __ Flowers   sachet, book, etc.)
                                       __ Other suggestions."

Suggestion:
1. To make your outline stronger,
    please make the 'Other suggestions' blank
    a little longer."

Question:

"1. Would a phone call be too off the beaten track
    from one or two of you on the *fourth* day,
        extemporaneous and quick,
    to tell me you'll be glad to see me back?
    And — let's suppose — I'm really *really* sick?
    Must I wait the week, full seven-day,
        to get my card, my book, sachet?"

Back to the outline,
    still under "ILLNESS":

2. Immediate Family
    A. In the Hospital
    __ Flowers   __ Toiletries
    __ Candy, etc.   __ Get well card
    __ Fruit   __ Other suggestions"-

Suggestions?
Just a question:

"1. Let's say, my son is hospitalized
    with an infected toe.
    Do *I* get the fruit or card,
        or toiletry?
    Or does he?
    I'd like to know — and why.
    (Or would a bad toe even qualify?)"

Next heading:

"DEATH
  1. Member
  ___ Flowers   ___ Card to family
  ___ Memorial   ___ Other suggestions"

Just thoughts and questions:

(I guess they mean *my* death, and so I wrote):

"My family doesn't know
about all your proposals and the vote.
They won't *expect* the flowers or the card;
if they don't get them, they won't take it hard.
But could a couple of you just drop by —
    informally —
to tell them you will miss me?
Or, maybe, send a little scribbled note?"
I added whimsically:
"If you feel you must send something when I die,
perhaps... the candy *here*? Or toiletry?
    Bath powder? Or cologne?
to perk them up a bit when I am gone?"

Still under DEATH, the outline carries on:

"2. Immediate Family
    A. Husband, Wife, Child, Mother, Father, Guardian
       Sister, Brother
___ Flowers   ___ Card of Sympathy
___ Telegram   ___ Other suggestons
___ Memorial

Again — just questions:

"1. If I lose my sister or my mother,
    try to understand,
  a little, caring touch from just one hand
    is all I ask for me.

Won't you try to see
that what helps is spontaneous and warm,
*un*outline-able in any form?"

The outline goes right on,
covering all occasions, all demands —
birth, wedding, retirement —
a teacher's full life span;
as outlines go, a truly paragon.

I really should commend
the Fellowship Committee, for they tried:
they did it, too — proposals, (classified),
for human kindnesses — clear-cut . . . just so,
all logical, efficient, simplified.

I *ought* to have commended them.
I should have shown them *that* much deference.

I couldn't though.
I didn't even check my preference.

But then, what do *I* know . . .
Me — confused, illogical, inept?

      And so . . .

I only put my head down on my desk
and — quite illogically — wept.

HE WHO LAUGHS LAST

This is *not* an "important" story, just let me say.
   (By the way, Muse,
      should you so choose to disavow
      this poet, for writing so shallowly now
      of rain puddles — in truth, *not* so shallow —
      and shoes.
   Then fly away, Muse.
      Who needs you, anyhow?)

My teacher friends demanded this one just for fun,
   because what befell
   afforded quite a few of them
   a laugh — (more than one or two of them).
   So to answer the cry and hue of them —
      this small, shallow story I tell.

(Oh — if anyone *can* dredge up something deep in it. DO!
   My hat, and the Muses' too,
      would certainly be off to you!)

It rained very early one day.
   A frog-strangler.
   A Biblical rain,
sloshing over my walk-way.

I was wearing my brand new shoes,
   my lovely Ruby Keeler-Ginger Rogers-Eleanor Powell-type
      tap-dance looking shoes,
   with ties over the instep and nice brown trim
      on slick shiny tan.
      That's not quite all . . .
   they made my size 9's look small.
      Wonderful shoes. Fun and fine.
         They cost me $5.99.

They were not made of leather.
Inside, it said: 'MAN-MADE MATERIAL,
MADE IN JAPAN."

When I arrived at school
 in that Biblical-rain-type weather,
 I sized up the Biblical puddles
 awash in the morning gloom.
 Quite naturally, using my head,
  (being nobody's fool),
 I shed my cardboard-type shoes,
 tucking them under my arm,
  (dryly, to keep them from harm,)
   and, tip-toe-like, ran
carrying them, with thermos and books, to my room.

Many and many a teachr sloshing to class
  in her sturdy, leather-type shoes,
   her "MADE IN AMERICA," $24.95-type shoes,
watched me, speedily tip-toeing wadefully shoeless,
splashing, just stockinged, along my watery way.

Guess WHO was the laugh of the teachers' lounge that day?

I couldn't quite *get* what all the mirth was about.
 My teacher friends tried to explain:
 "Shoes," they patiently pointed out,
  protect your stockings and feet from rain.
  Shoes are to keep ON. See?"

Up there at the lounge, they thought what I'd done
 quite naturally — quite odd.
 Why, they'd just leap on me,
 laughing and carrying on
 at my shoeless promenade
 when I'd even go *near* the place.

And still they laugh, to this day.

Me — I still am wearing those shoes,
   (still nice, still together),
     whenever I choose —
   in puddle-free weather.
And *I'M* laughing louder than they,
   from the other side of my face.

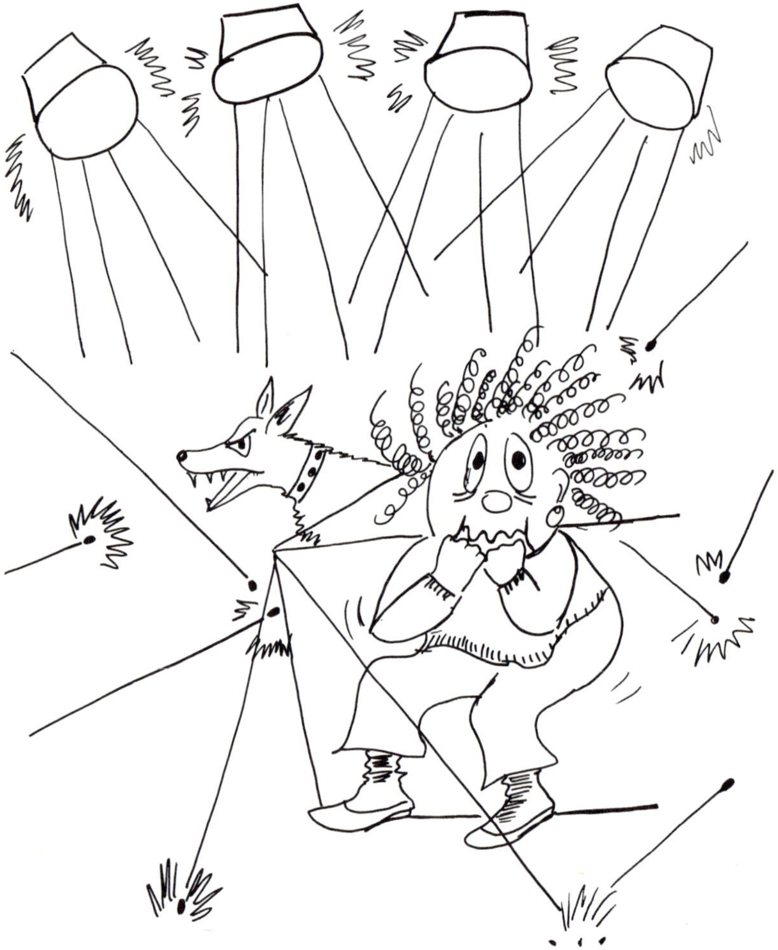

MY! AREN'T THEY *BRIGHT*!?

There had settled soft upon my room at school
a certain, lovely glow.

It was not *always* so.

We have fluorescent light
   in long, white skinny tubes,
      row after row,
   up on the ceiling.
It is — at *full* strength — harsh,
   brutally bright,
   imparting to the room all the charm
      of a factory,
      or the third-degree.
It gives you an unrelaxed feeling.

It is not friendly.

One of those tubes over where I sit
   high-lighted the circles under my eyes.
The little spots on my desk were well-lit,
   where my ball point
     and thermos
       leaked.

But two of mine had, happily, burned out —
   the one over me,
   one toward the back.
Two others flickered a lot.
Oh . . . you could still see,
   but it was cozier . . .
     with atmosphere.
Report them to the custodian for repair
   I did not.

But after Christmas, when I returned
    and flicked on the switch,
    BLASTING down, a million kilowatts burned,
        drowning me in suffocating glare.
I crouched, waiting to hear shrieking sirens,
        snarling German shepherds,
        th rat-tat-tat of machine guns;
Every inch of that room — flooded with the paralyzing presence,
        the penetrating luminesence
        of ruthless, relentless fluorescense.

As I cowered, whimpering, behind my file,
    the custodian poked in his head,
    in the middle of which — a big proud smile.

        "How d'ya like your lights?" he beamed.
        "I fixed 'em for ya!" he said.

"Yes!
You certainly did fix them, all right.
My! Aren't they *bright!*"

And now, I do not like my room so much.
It looks like all the other rooms.
All the little bad things show up:
    dust . . .
        smudgy spots . . .
        my circles . . .
        the four-letter words on the desks, and such.

But I am trying to grow up,
    accept how things turned out;
    accept the harsh lights of reality,
        the probing luminesence,
            their permeating presence . . .
    and wait — just patiently —
    'til some of my fluorescents
        have, once again,
            happily,
            burned out.

THE TRIP

We took our leave on Saturday, A.M.,
  with time to spare.
How happy ... proud I was when we got there
  and walked together into that big room
  where eager, young, aspiring writers stood,
  waiting for the Workshop to begin.
Our entourage of seventeen
  was three — or maybe even four — times more
  than any other.
     Then, too,
I was very grateful; each of you
  had given up your Saturday
  to listen, grow; and if you could
  to learn to write things better than before.

A beautiful young poet was our seer.
We listened — spellbound —
  as she talked to us of sight
     and sound;
  and how to make another *feel*
  things we have felt ... and found;
  and how to make our writing *real* ...
     and new.

How happy, then, I was to be with you
  in the college lecture room that day
  as you wrote of things ... and made them true;
  and with the way you looked around
  a little shyly ... not a little proud,
  acknowledging soft smiles I sent your way
  as the poet read *your* words aloud.

But lunch break came.
     I lost you, then.
I — with the older ones.
You — among yourselves.

Thinking back now, I suppose
I should have stayed with you.
We had an hour or more.
    What happened?
    Did you get restless? Bored?

You barely just got back that afternoon.
You bunched together on the last two rows.
    I sat further down.
    I didn't say, "Move closer!"
    I didn't scold . . . or frown.

The giggles — at first — I just ignored.
    But pretty soon
I turned around and lightly wagged a finger
at the buzzing, giggling crowd of you.
    You only giggled more.
I didn't want to know it; but I knew.
    You were high on pot.
    You do not giggle like that when you're not.

While you tripped off in *your* world — apart,
That beautiful young poet spun for us
    such sparkling, new adventures with her art
    that I was tumbled, tossed
    among the stars on carpets woven bright
    with searing, soaring sounds.
    She led me to new heights
    of true experience with sights
    she delicately painted there for me
    with every perfect word.

But you, young friends, were lost,
    away out on your funny, phony trip . . .
    and never even heard.

IT WAS HERE NOT THREE DAYS AGO!

Yesterday I went to Ms. B's room.
She teaches Hemingway,
  (who somebody in my class was . . .
  make that — *whom* —
  whom somebody was doing a paper on.)
I asked her did she have a folder on him?
I could tell right off she did, and knew where it was . . .
                 because
           not blinking an eye,
            she rose, straightway,
         from her neat, neat desk,
       eyes shining, shoulders squared,
               undaunted . . .
                 prepared,
and walked — make that . . . *strode* . . . to her file.
          No fooling around.
     She hit that "H" drawer and found,
          in her very first try,
    the folder on Ernest Hemingway.
       Briskly pulling it out,
     precisely tucking in loose ends,
    (which there weren't any of),
      with a smug little smile,
     and a neat little shove,
     smartly slamming her file,
      making sort of a bow,
    she handed it over to me.
     I let slip with a big, dumb:
           "WOW!"
     Then tried to cover up some,
        as well as I could,
   with a casual, "Thanks. Very good.
       That's just fine."

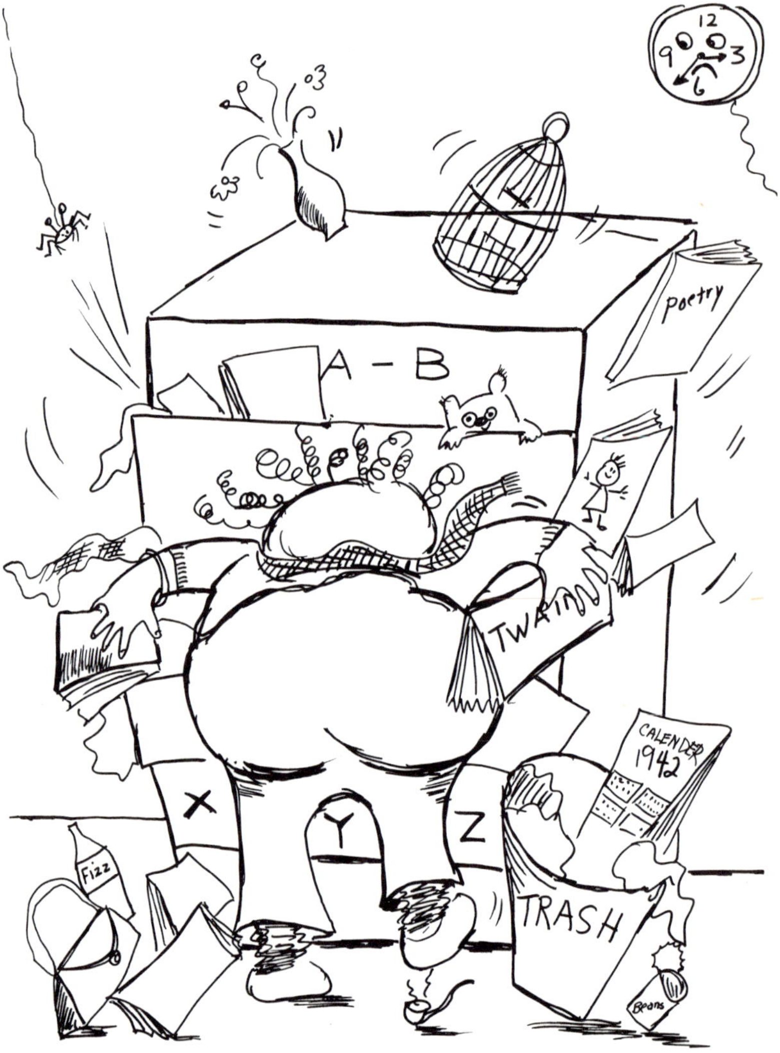

12
9
3
6
A - B
Poetry
TWAIN
CALENDER
1942
X
Y
Z
Fizz
TRASH
Beans

Now I can only pray
   that she may never come
   to ask for *my* folder on Truman Capote,
   who I taught...
   make that — *whom* I taught sometime last May.
Because if she comes for the stuff,
          I will go for the bluff,
          but right off, she will surmise
          that all is *not* well.
    From my piled up-and-up desk, she can tell,
        and from the way I arise,
        wobbly... wavering.
   She will already know before I get *near* that file...
        it'll be a while.
She will know by my unsteady gait,
      my thin little smile,
      my face, flushed and hot,
      that she's in for a wait;
and that *her* guess as to Truman Capote's whereabouts
      is as good as mine.
      No — not as good;
      she'll think he's in the "C's."
      She'll be out of line.
      I'm quite sure he's *not*.

I will try to remember her stride,
   as she bee-lined it for those "H's" that day
   so primly self-satisified.
I will try to do it that way.
          I will fail.
She will know, as I falter file-ward,
   that I am *not* at ease,
   trembling and pale,
   as I hopefully — (but not very) —
   hit that drawer with the "C's,"
   soon stooping to fling out drawer after drawer...
          after drawer.
And before Ms. B can count to a thousand
   I'll have plowed through the "D's,"

　　　　　the "P.s"....
　　　　　the "Z's"....
　　　　　and more.

Dumping folders, papers, and God-knows-*what*-all aside,
　　　　I will mumble softly:
　　　　"I'm SURE it is here. You know
　　　　I saw that folder not three days ago!"

I will sense,
　　watching, peripherally —
　　as she shifts her weight,
　　clears and clears her throat,
　　　　pushing papers aside,
　　so she can tap on my desk nervously;
I will — somehow — sense
　　her mounting impatience...
　　and even — dismay —
　　with my filing "system"... and me.

Since I'm caught, I'll cut the pretense,
　　I will, then, in self-defense,
　　gently suggest that she go.
　　"I will send it to you. You know
　　I saw that folder in here...
　　　　barely three... four days ago!"

And what do you know?
　　Three and one-half weeks hence,
　　when I am looking for my file for Mark Twain,
　　　there'll be good old Truman Capote,
　　　right in there with the "R's."
I will briskly send it to her...
　　three-and-one-fourth weeks too late;
　　she's gone on to Faulkner,
　　　or James, or Lewis, Sinclair,
　　who *whom*, I note, she did NOT request
　　　　that I look up for her...
　　　　which is really too bad,
　　　because they're *all* ones I had...
　in that file of mine... there...
　　　　　SOMEwhere!

FROM THE FANTASIES OF A NOT-SO-YOUNG-ANYMORE SCHOOL TEACHER

There's a lot of things I've done
In my small spot in the sun;
I have not sat and let life pass me by.
Once, I even led a line
That was perfect, straight, and fine.
Now! There's one more thing I *really* want to try.

The dream that I have planned
Is to lead a marching band
Down a football field some chilly autumn night.
The cheers will keep me warm
In my little uniform —
All blue and silver, shimmery and tight.

The bleachers will be rocking.
(I will wear elastic stockings,
 So the veins in my old legs will hardly show.)
I will strut and prance and shake,
'Til the stadium will quake,
As the trumpets and the frosty breezes blow.

With my whistle, clear and shrill,
I will call a fancy drill;
And I'll toss my bright baton up in the air.
Being careful not to drop it,
I will twirl and twist and flop it,
Running circles 'round MY BAND . . . and everywhere.

I will march so straight and tall
They will find no fault at all
With their majorette of forty-some odd years.
With my stomach held in tight,
As my sequins catch the light,
I will smile and blow some kisses at their cheers.

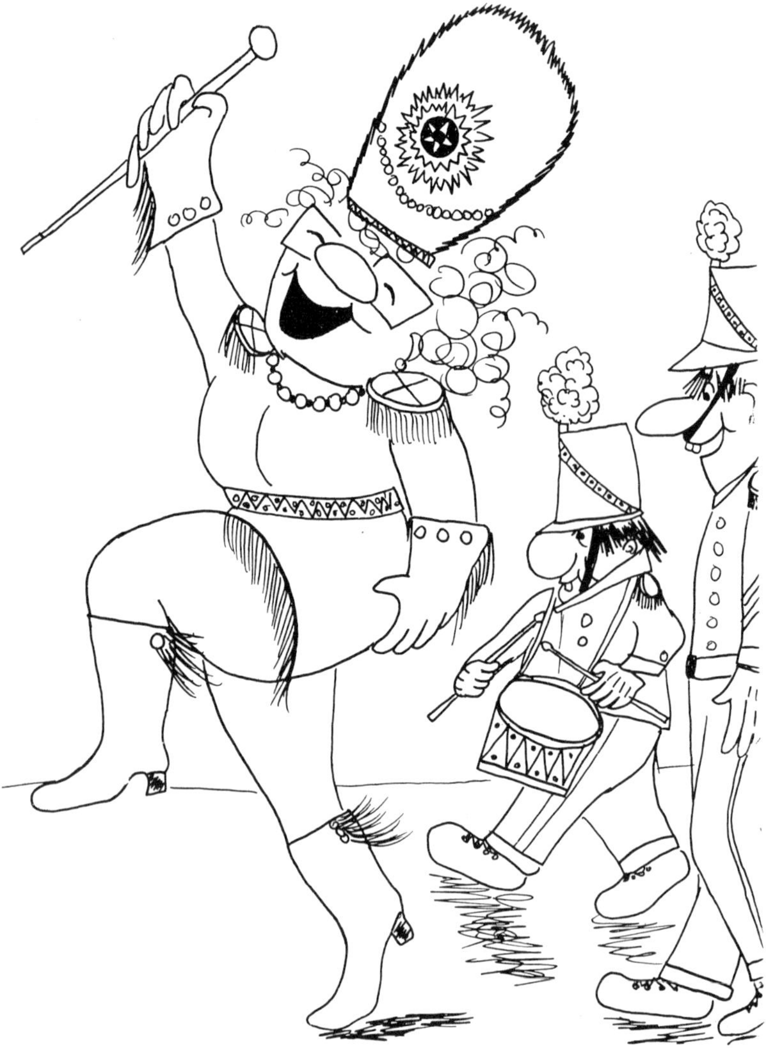

'Til the half-time show is done,
I will strut and skip and run
With a ZIP they never dreamed I could display.
Then they'll yell: "SOMEBODY – *CATCH* HER!"
As they hurry with the stretcher
    To carry me – triumphantly – away!

"EXCUSE THE INTERRUPTION, PLEASE..."

The "Teachable Moment."
You've heard about it.
You wonder how it happens.
 Why? When? Where?
And if it comes, how can you tell?

Suddenly ... one day ... it's there!

You're reading aloud.
The words begin to cast a spell:

"The great red hills stand desolate and the earth has torn
away like flesh. The lightning flashes over them..."

They listen to the magical, musical words;
 they really *hear*...

"... the clouds pour down upon them, the dead streams come
to life full of the red blood of the earth. Down in the valleys..."

"EXCUSE THE INTERRUPTION, PLEASE.
WILL ALL THE CONTESTANTS FOR THE 'MISS HOMEMAKER BAKE-OFF
CONTEST' REPORT TO THE HOME EC. ROOM IMMEDIATELY?..."

You hesitate ... then struggle on ...
 "... women scratch the soil that is left, and ..."

"BE SURE, CONTESTANTS, TO BRING YOUR APRONS AND YOUR RECIPES..."

Hold the magic!
Don't stop now ...

 "...and the maze hardly reaches..."

"THE FOLLOWING STUDENTS ARE TO BE EXCUSED. TEACHERS, PLEASE PERMIT
THEM TO LEAVE YOUR CLASS IF THEY ARE NOT TAKING A TEST:
MARY ANN JONES, ALICE VANDERMERE, CONNIE GREEN..."

  and on...
  and on...
  and on......
Quietly, you close the book.
The "Moment," the magic, all of it — gone.
  gone...
  gone...
  gone.......

Finally, you still your sophomores —
restless, twittering class.
If this side of the room isn't giggling, whispering,
 that side is.

You've shouted. And pleaded. And stared.
Up 'til this moment, nobody listened. Or cared.
 But now the buzzing has ebbed,
  ebbed and faded. It's there!
You begin. Everything's right.
This is it!
You explain about you...
 about them.
What it's about.
Why they are here.
 The outlook's bright.
 The breakthrough's near.

BUT.......

"EXCUSE THE INTERRPUTION, PLEASE.
THE FOLLOWING STUDENTS WILL REPORT TO THE
GYM FOR MAKE-UP PICTURES."

And while the reachable, "Teachable Moment"
 remains, for a few, receding seconds, suspended in air,
 while you stand only inches from igniting the light,
  evoking the voice within,

that voice *without*
proceeds to shout seventeen names.
Along about nine or ten,
  the tittering, the giggling,
  the hassles pick up and grow
  into a tidal wave.
Too late to save
  the Magic Moment.
You know you've lost it — again.

Finally, the shy young man has ventured
  to stand, unsteadily, at the lecturn
  to share with us his story about a boy and his dog.
He speaks, his voice a frail craft,
    dipping, wavering, trembling . . .
    then gaining strength as he finds we're with him. . .
    calmer, stronger, surer . . .

"EXCUSE THE INTERRUPTION, PLEASE.
THERE IS A GREEN AND WHITE MAZDA BLOCKING MRS. BLACKSMITH'S
CAR IN THE TEACHER'S PARKING LOT. IT MUST BE MOVED IMMEDIATELY."

Three students loudly leap for the door.
Others laugh.
  The spell is broken.
  The bickering begins
    and builds into a mighty roar.
The young narrator, shattered,
  flees to his desk, his moment gone,
    most likely — forevermore.

So it goes — on and on.

"EXCUSE THE INTERRPUTION, PLEASE.
ALL BUS DRIVERS REPORT TO THE OFFICE."

"EXCUSE THE INTERRUPTION, PLEASE.
CINDY LOU INGRAM HAS LOST A BLACK AND GREEN WALLET."

"EXCUSE THE INTERRUPTION, PLEASE."
DO NOT USE THE RESTROOMS. THE WATER HAS BEEN TURNED OFF."

"EXCUSE THE INTERRUPTION, PLEASE..."

"EXCUSE, PLEASE..."

"EXCUSE...."

    PLEASE....

Oh.... PLEASE.... PLEASE...

      P   L E A S E..........

Lines are quoted from *Cry the Beloved Country* by Alan Paton.

I must commend the administration at North Mecklenburg High School for the extent to which they have curtailed the interruption of classes. The intercom is used sparingly. I include this poem because of "popular request" from teachers at other schools.

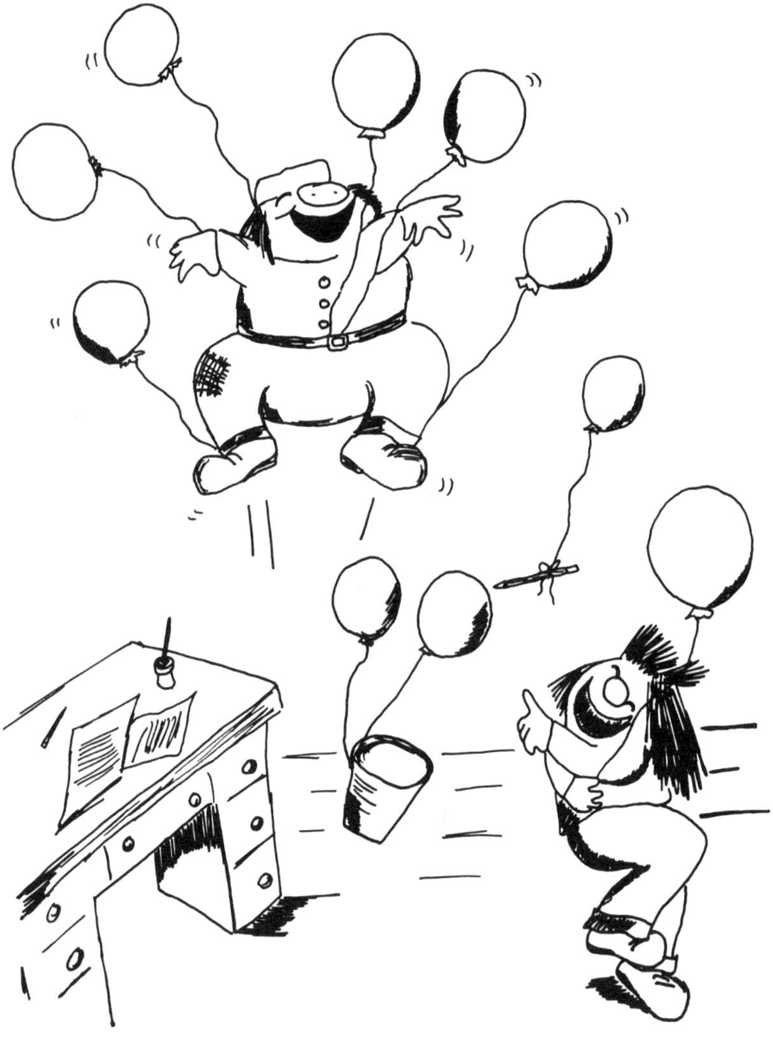

WHO SAID TODAY'S KIDS DON'T HAVE FEELING?!???

A Booster Club person
brought some
BALLOONS —
bobbing . . . blue . . . bright —
not filled with air,
but with helium,
into my first-period class.
And there . . .
in my room . . .
at 8:11 A.M.,
wonderful things occurred.
Incredible sight:
sleep-soggy, limp young lumps
stirred . . .
BURSTING awake,
and jumped,
making the fast break
for that Blue-Balloon Person.

I mean — even the kids who are pretty tight
times we collect for the sick, or — like that,
right off the bat,
(and just about everyone),
tossed out coins left and right
for BALLOON-kind-of-fun.

The Balloon Person had to go back and back again
for more of those bright, bouncy spheres.

One young man bought eight of them,
carefully tying them on to his hat
and shoes and belt and ears.
(He was ballooned fore . . . and aft.)

Oh . . . I wish *you'd* been there at barely past dawn
to see
those cool, turned-off Dudes turn ON,
doing their tricks,
like children of six,
they squealed . . . and giggled . . . and LAUGHED!

Pretty soon,
someone cut off the end of one.
Inhaling the air in a gulp,
he talked in that Minnie Mouse voice you talk in
when you gulp the insides of a balloon.

They tied little things
to those blue orbs,
happily watching pencils and chalk take wings
and bob on up to the ceiling.

I just want to know:
Who SAID today's kids don't have *feeling*?!?????

Oh sure . . . the Balloon Affair
destroyed my lesson plans.
But I didn't care.
It was O.K.,
because . . . afterwards — somehow —
I felt so GOOD about . . . things
for the rest of the day.
And still . . . even now!